Yogi Bean Books ©

'DEITY, an Adult Coloring Book to Invoke the Divine'

ISBN-13: 978-1545156810

ISBN-10: 1545156816

. my family .

DEITY

an Adult Coloring Book to Invoke the Divine

DANU

[dah-noo]

Danu, the Celtic mother goddess of wisdom,

protection, abundance, fertility and magic.

To invoke Danu, recite:

"Danu, The Goddess of Earthly Magic, I Salute You."

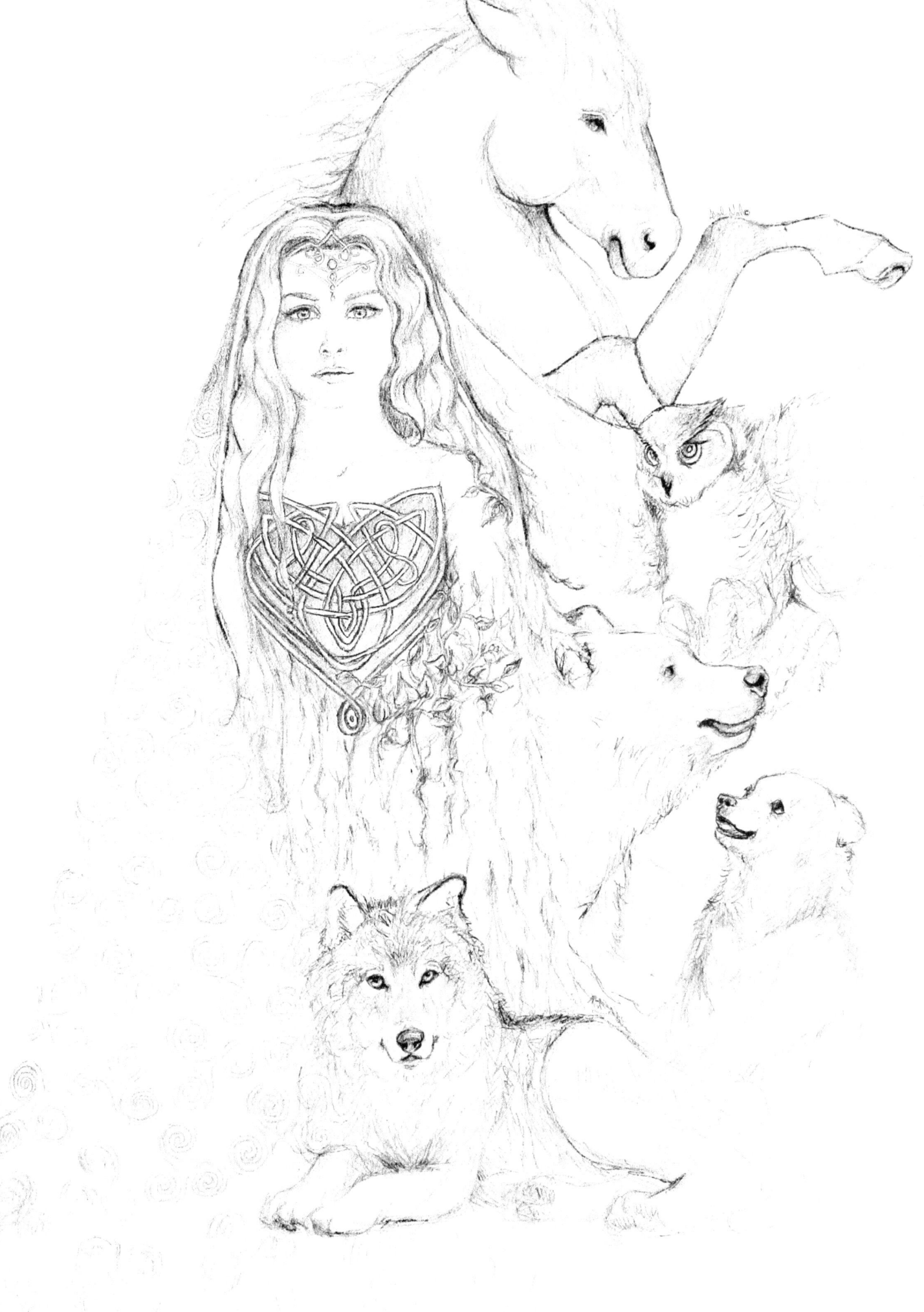

KUAN YIN

[kwan-jin]

Kuan Yin, Chinese depiction, exemplifies love and mercy.

She is the goddess of health, fertility, compassion and kindness.

To invoke Kuan Yin, recite:

"Om Mani Padme Hum."

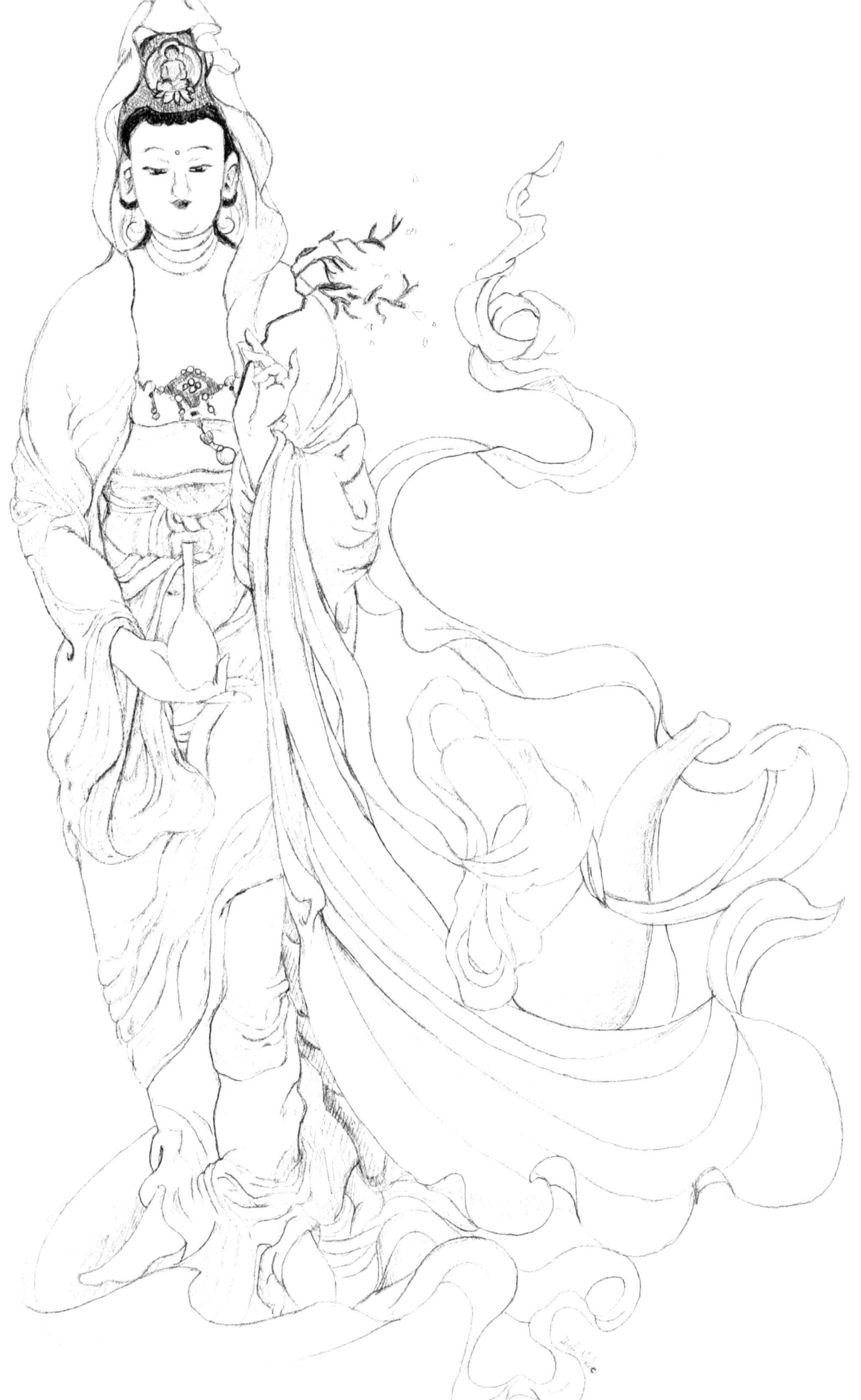

KUAN YIN

[kwan-jin]

Kuan Yin, Tibetan depiction, is also known as Avalokiteshvara.

She is the goddess of compassion. She helps all who suffer.

To invoke Kuan Yin, recite:

"Om Mani Padme Hum."

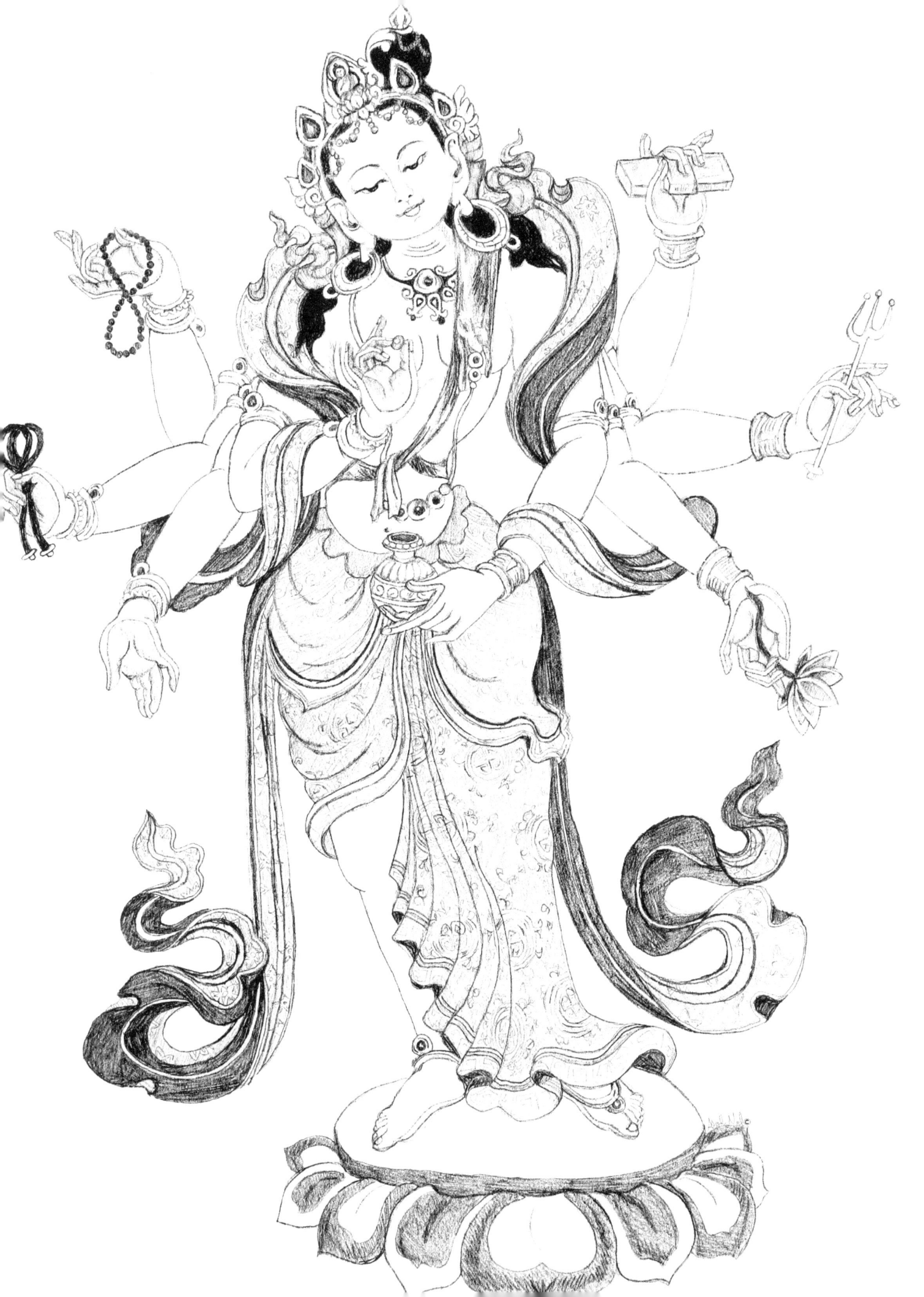

GANESHA

[guh-ney-shuh]

Ganesha, represents the remover of obstacles

and a god of new beginnings.

To invoke Ganesha, recite:

"Om Gam Ganapataye Namaha."

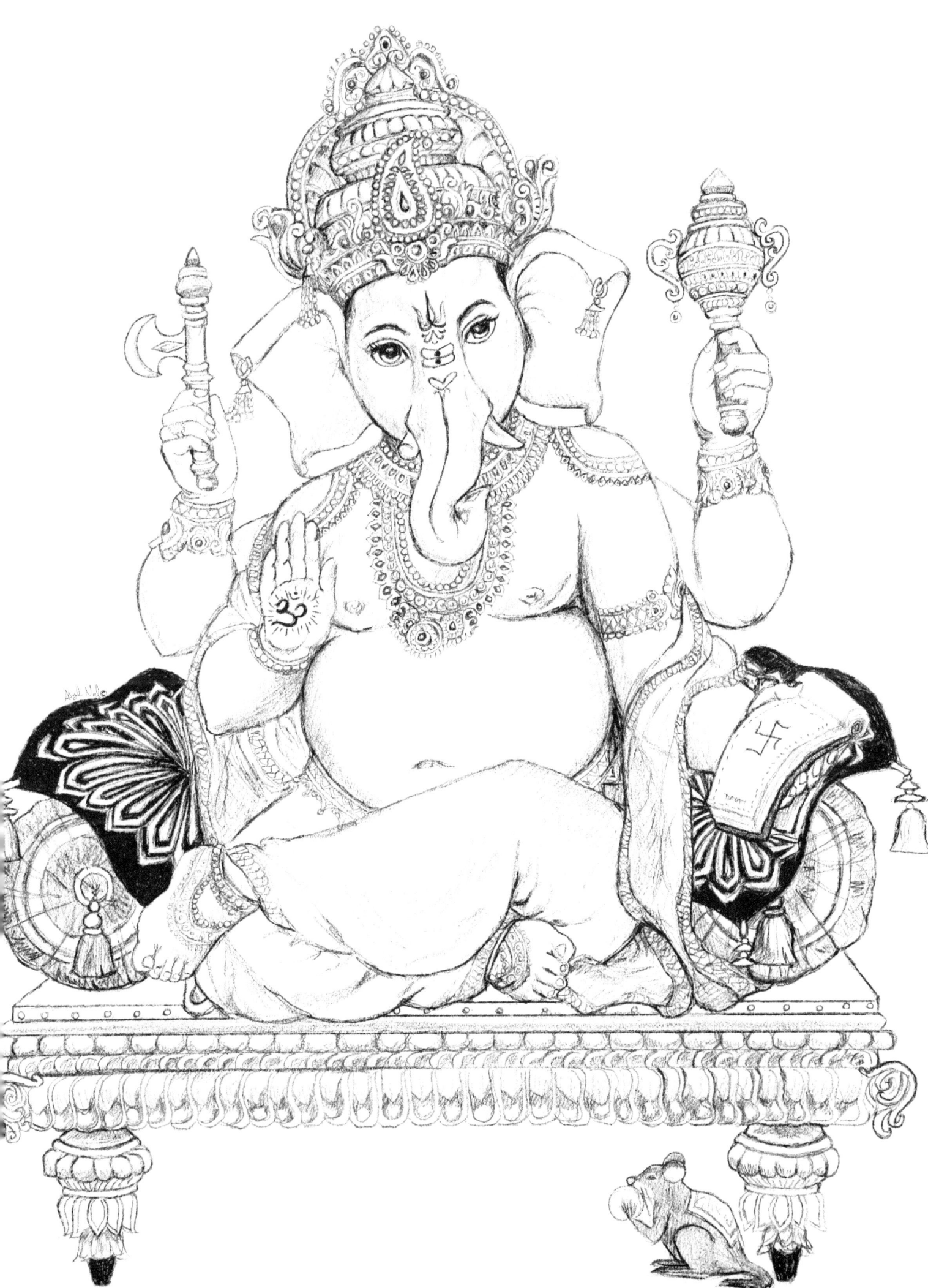

DURGA

[door-gah]

Durga, is the goddess symbolizing power and strength

in Hindu mythology- evil can not access her.

To invoke Durga, recite:

"Om Dum Durgayai Namah."

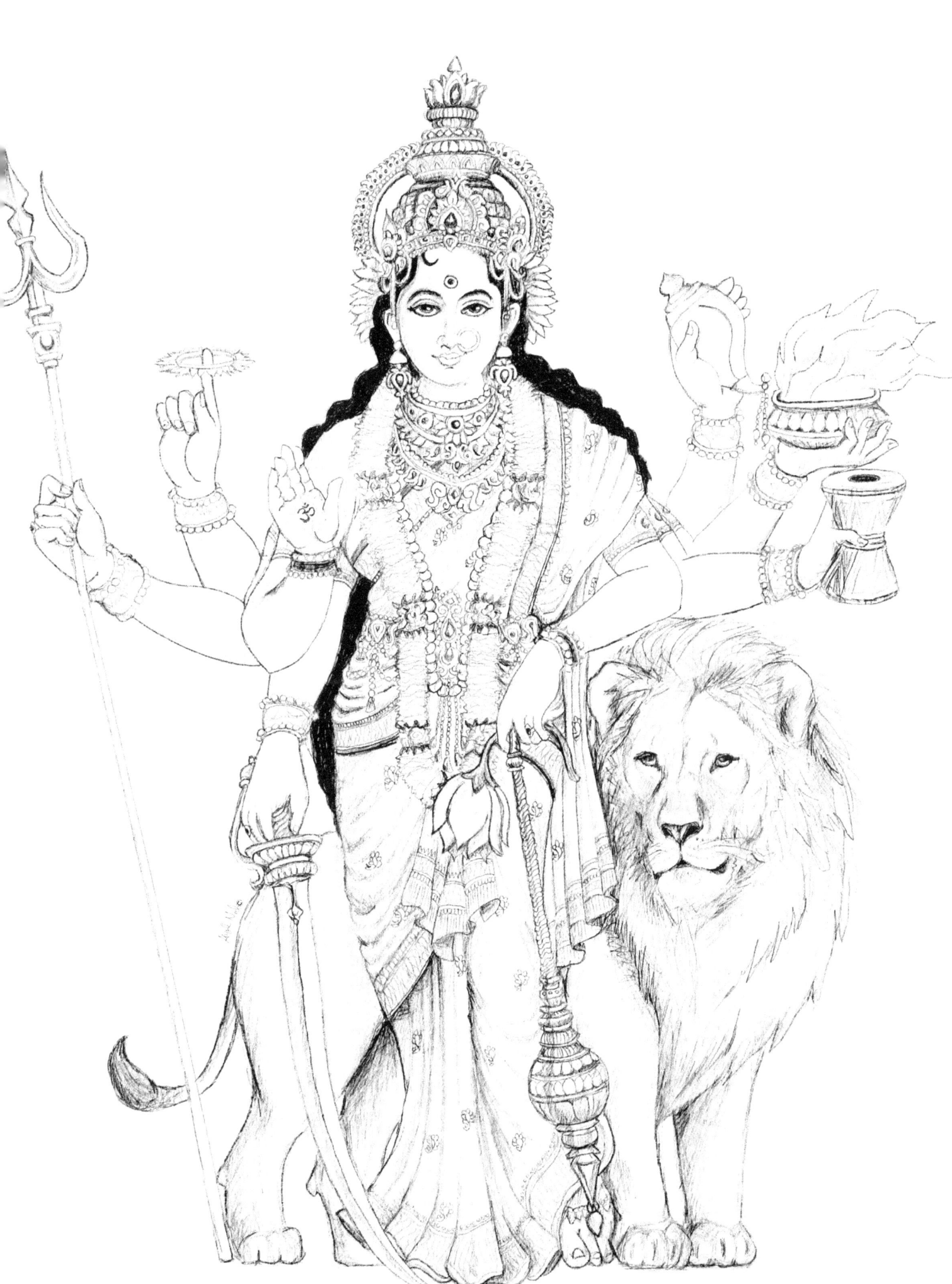

VISHNU

[vish-noo]

Vishnu, is known as the preserver, protector

and maintainer of cosmic order in the universe,

in Hindu mythology. He is a guide in troubled times,

and restores the balance of good and evil.

To invoke Vishnu, recite:

"Om Kleem Vishnave Namah."

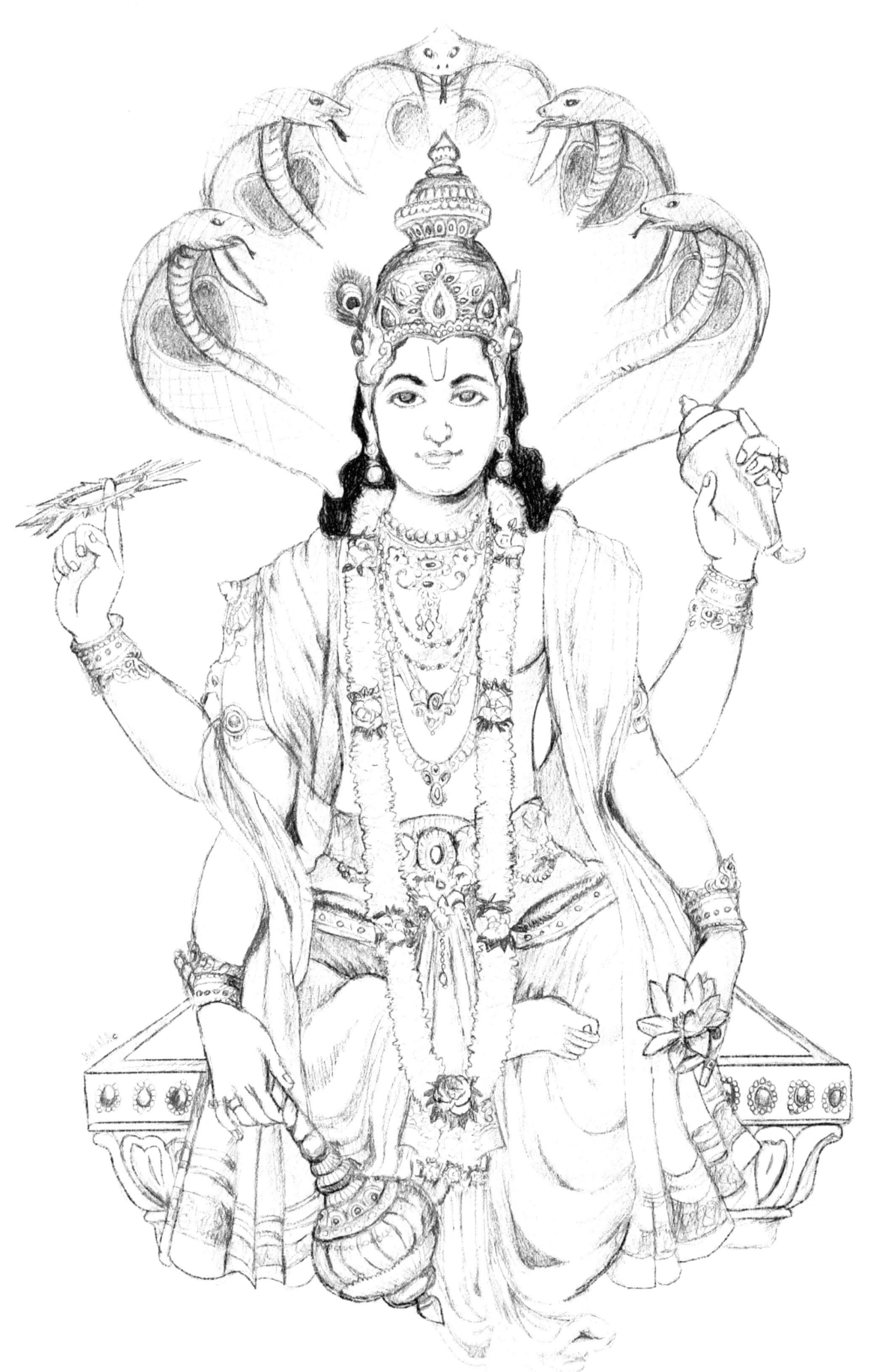

KRISHNA

[krish-nuh]

Krishna, embodies innocence, charm, purity

and beauty in male form. He exemplifies high

moral ground and is understood as the preserver

of natural order in Hindu mythology.

To invoke Krishna, recite:

"Om Krishnaya Namah."

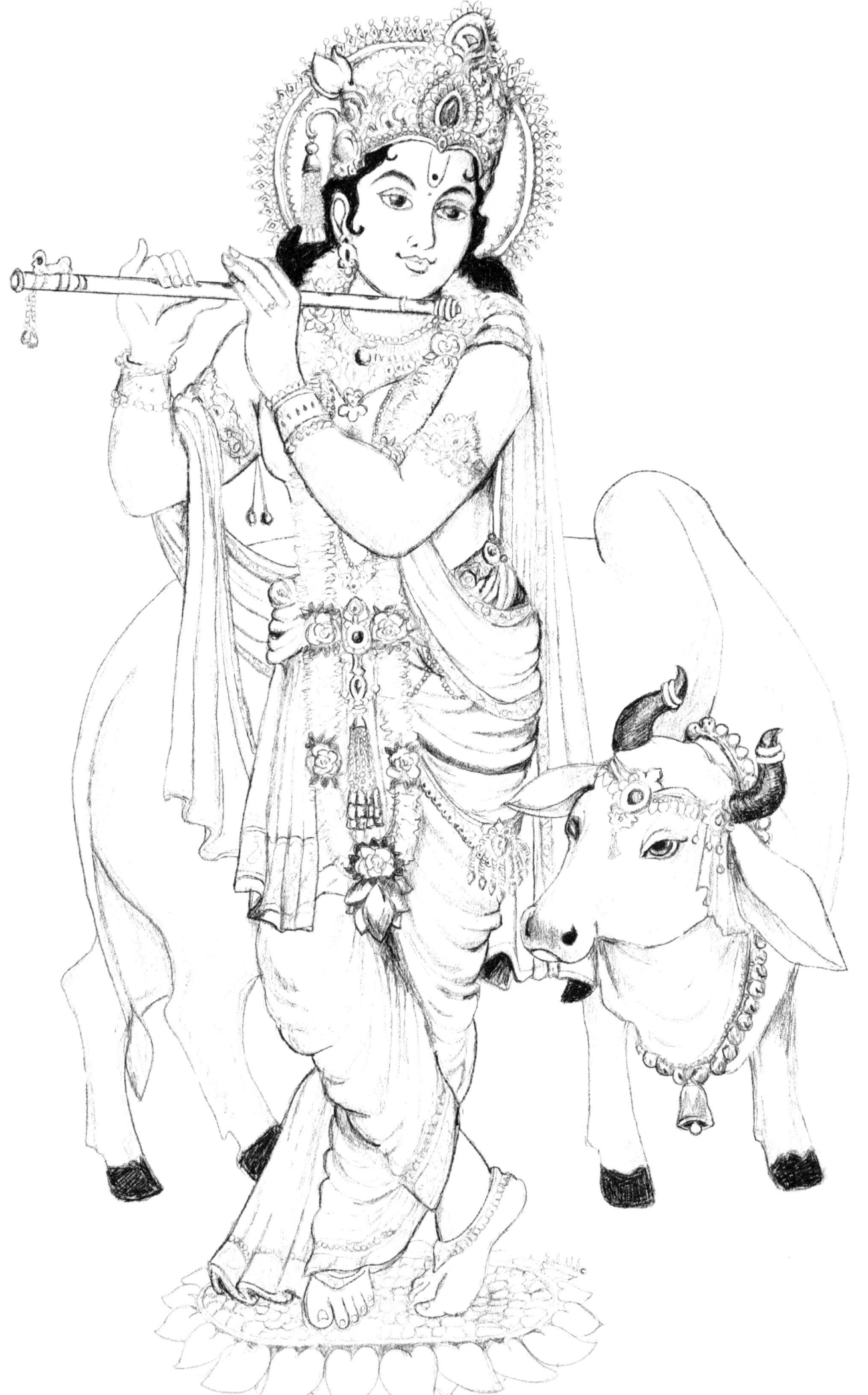

SARASWATI

[suh-ruhs-vuh-tee]

Saraswati, is the goddess of everything that flows;

knowledge, wisdom, music and the arts.

To invoke Saraswati, recite:

"Om Sam Sarasvatyai Namah."

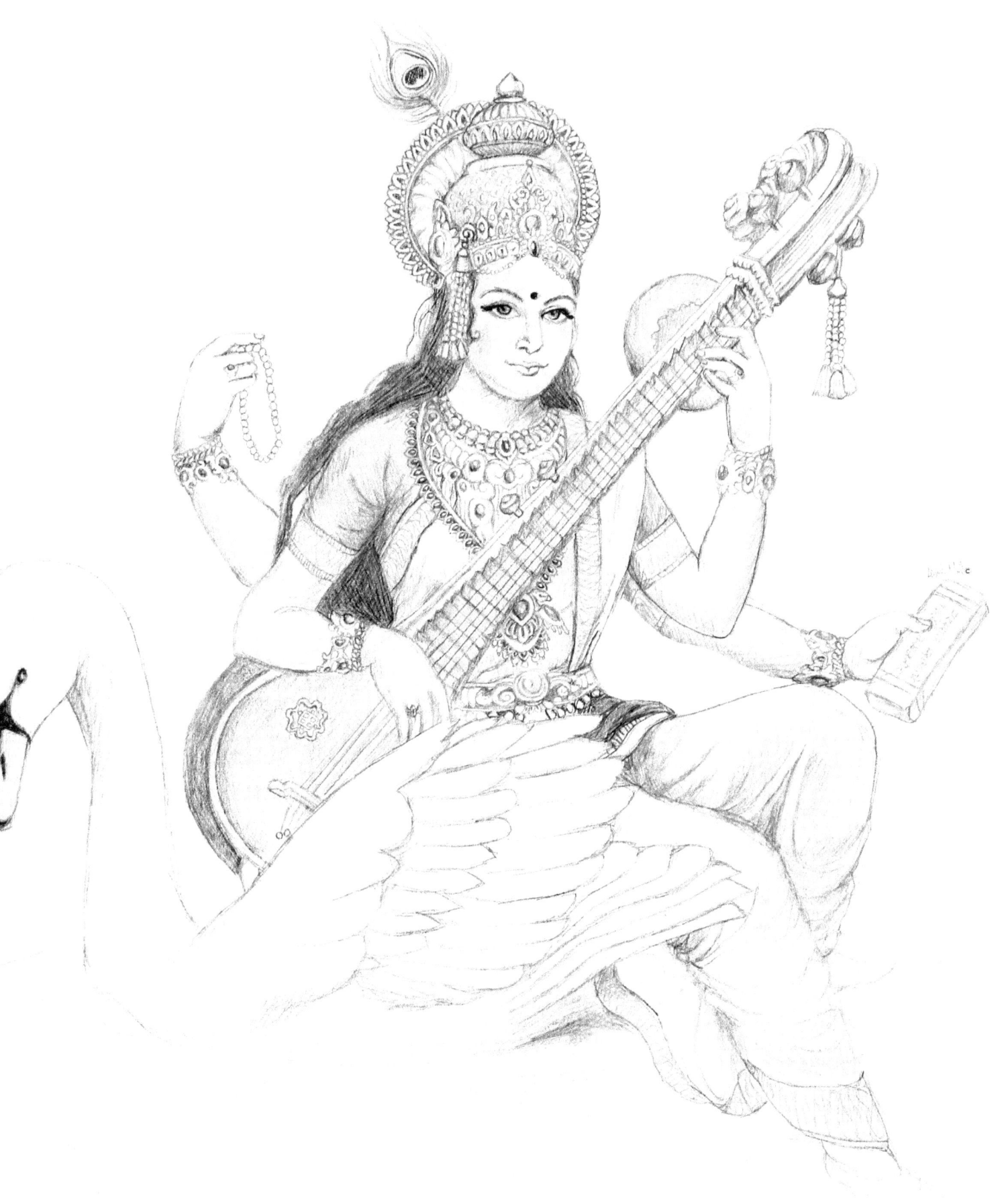

GANESHA

[guh-ney-shuh]

Ganesha, represents the remover of obstacles

and a god of new beginnings.

To invoke Ganesha, recite:

"Om Gam Ganapataye Namaha."

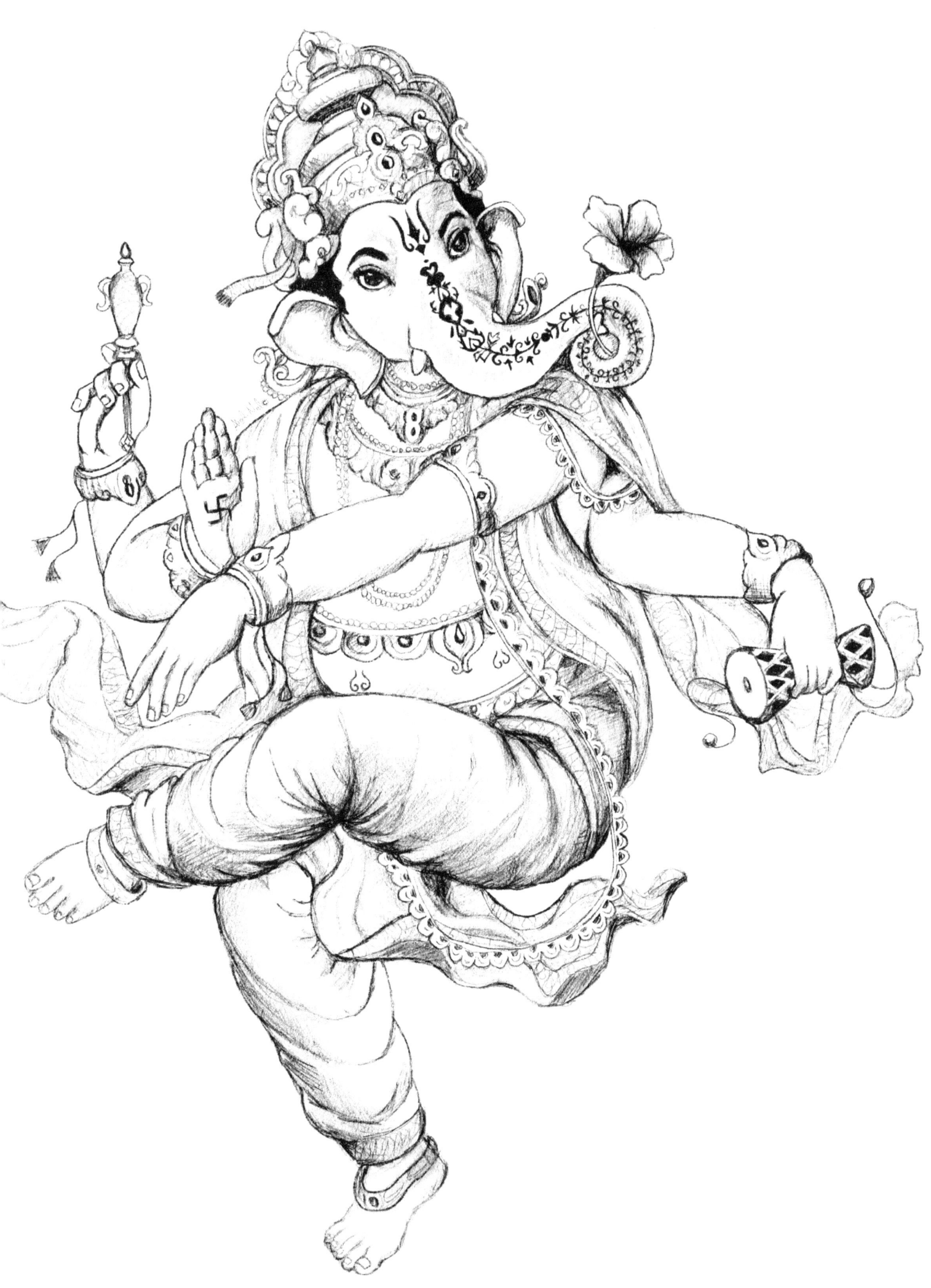

LAKSHMI

[luhksh-mee]

Lakshmi, is the goddess of wealth, prosperity

and abundance in the Hindu mythology.

To invoke Lakshmi, recite:

"Om Shreem Laksmyai Namah."

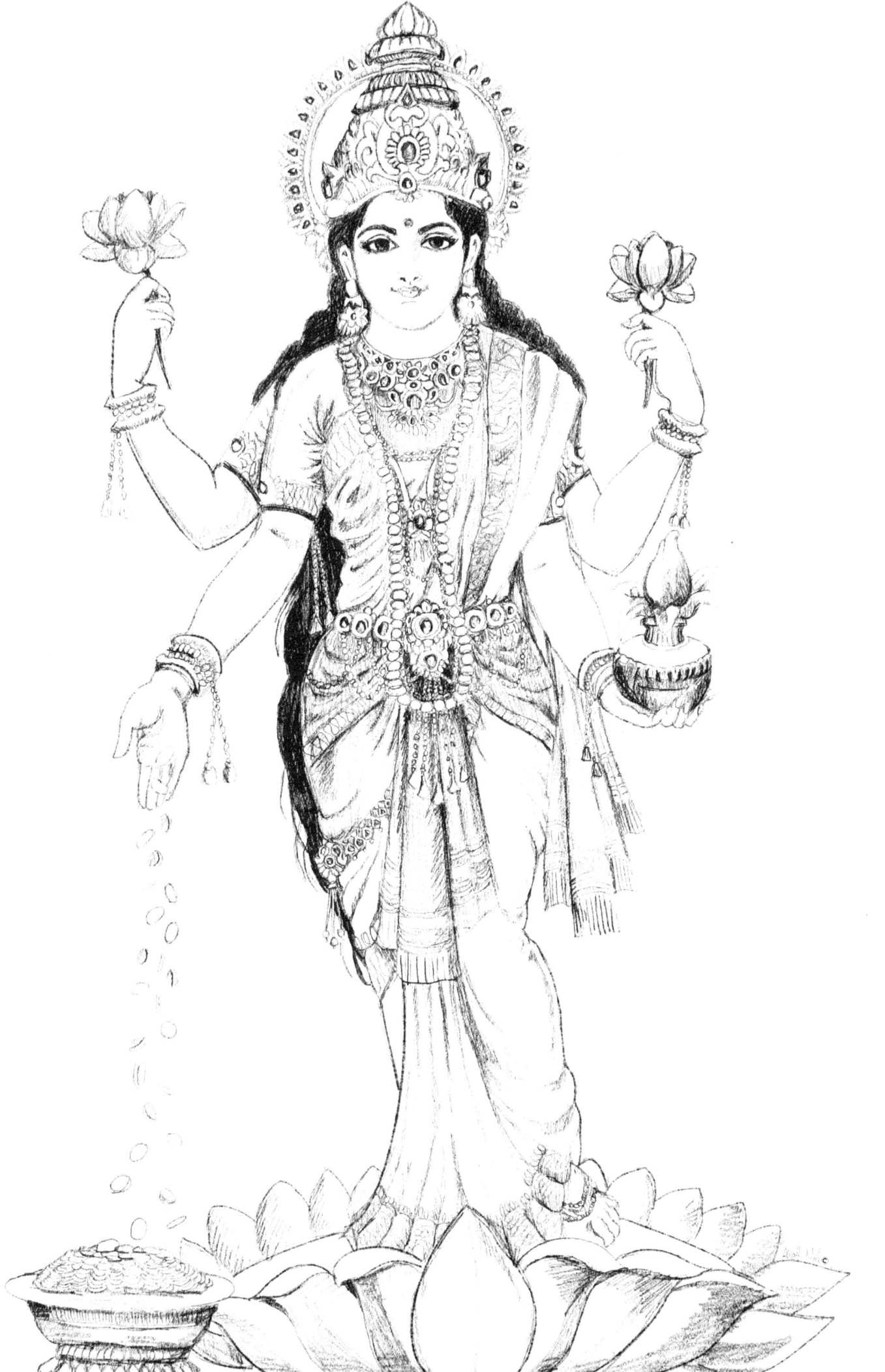

HANUMAN

[huhn-oo-mahn]

Hanuman, is the Monkey God in Hindu mythology.

He represents the strength of love and devotion gained

from being aligned with a greater purpose.

To invoke Hanuman, recite:

"Om Hanumate Namah."

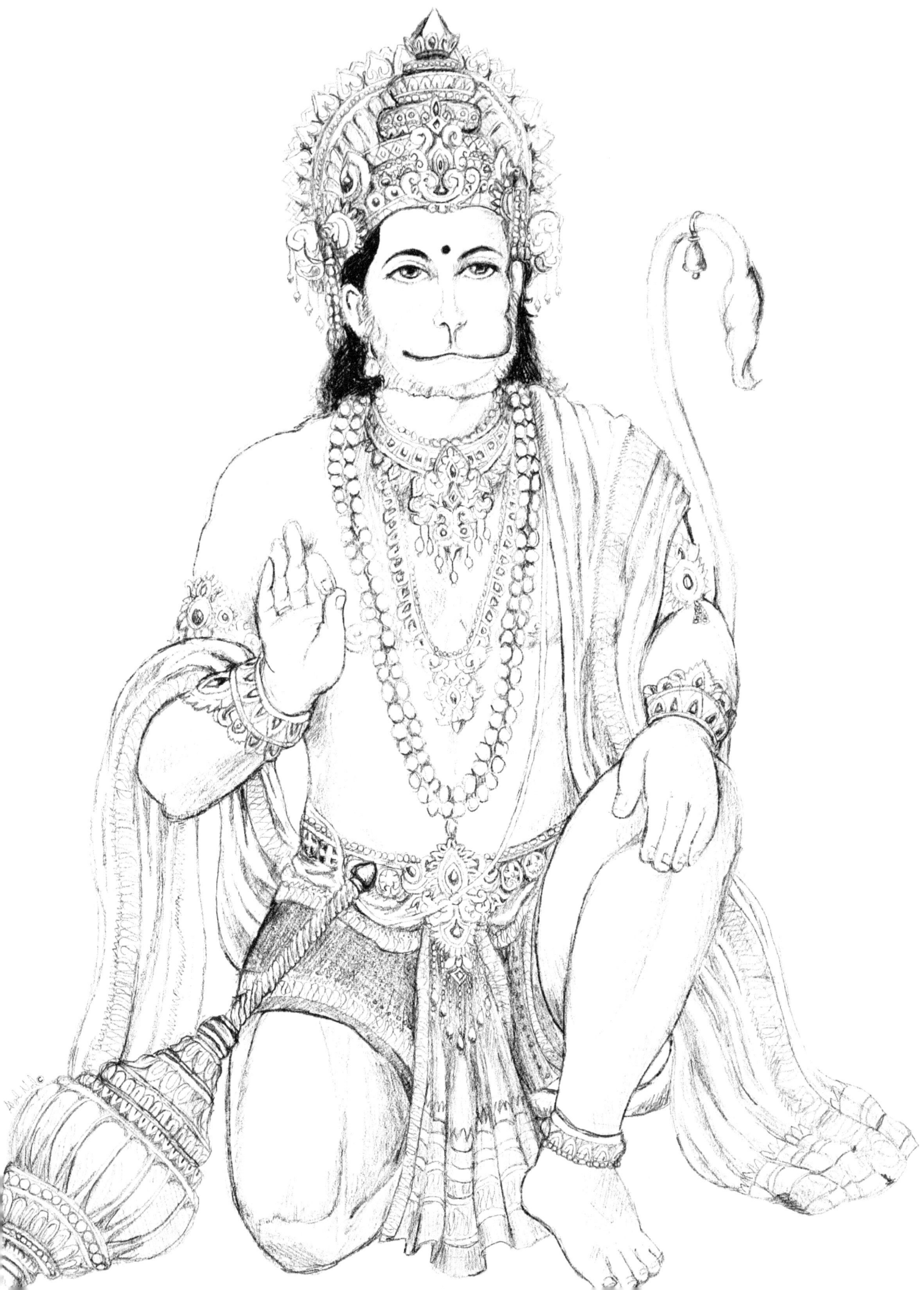

SHIVA

[shee-vuh]

Shiva, is the embodiment of the silent, subtle

and infinite qualities in nature.

He is the founder of yoga, the first Yogi.

To invoke Shiva, recite:

"Om Namha Shivaya."

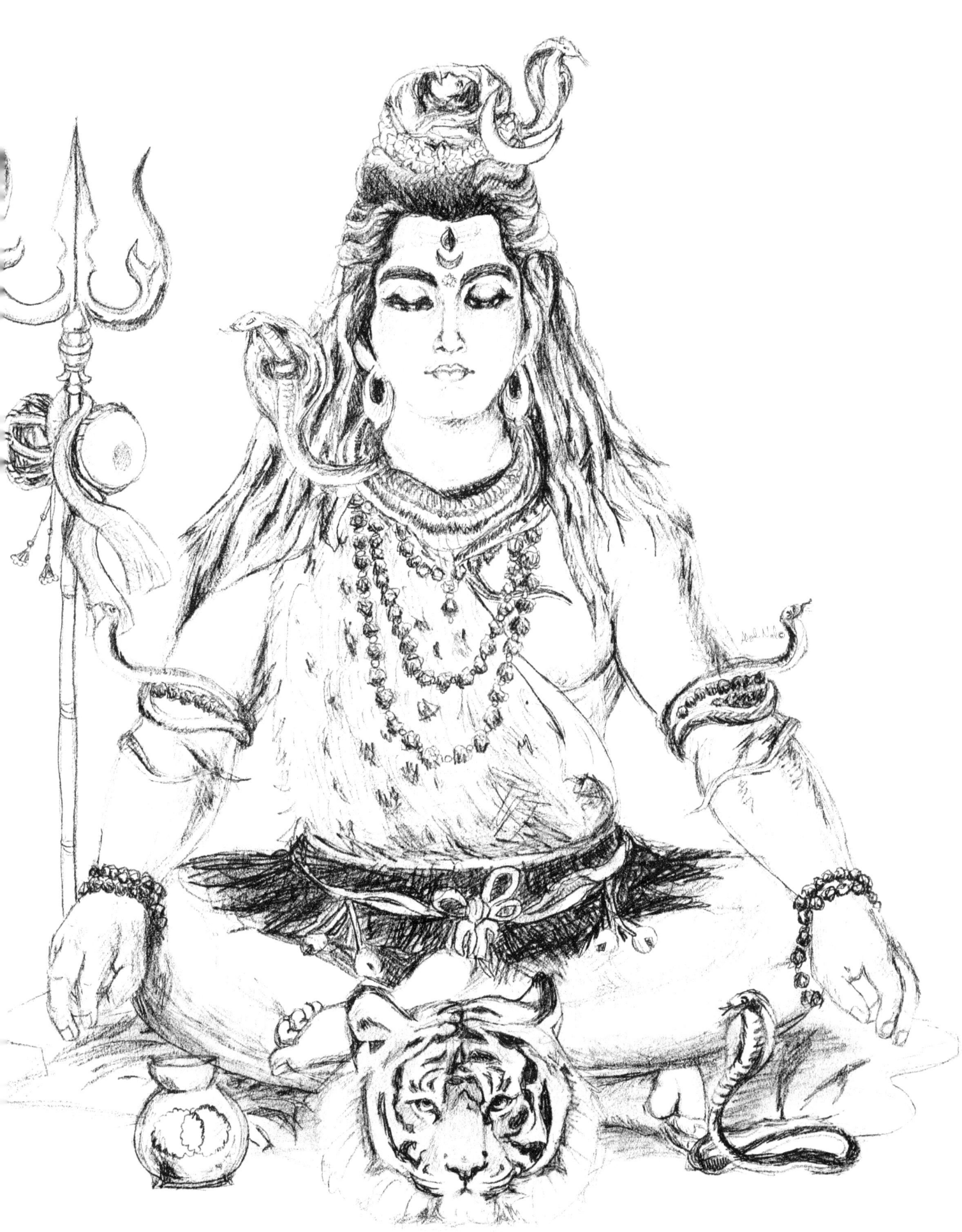

About the Author

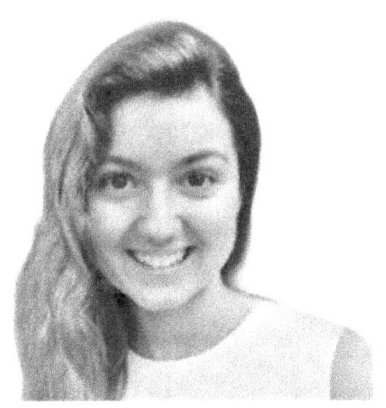

Abigail Neal

Author and Illustrator of the Yogi Bean series,
'Yogi Bean, The Quest to Sprout.' She is a
practitioner of Ayurveda, Herbalist and
a student of Yoga. Each of her Yogi Bean
publications aims to bring more peace to the world.

Any questions? Email us!
YogiBeanBooks@gmail.com